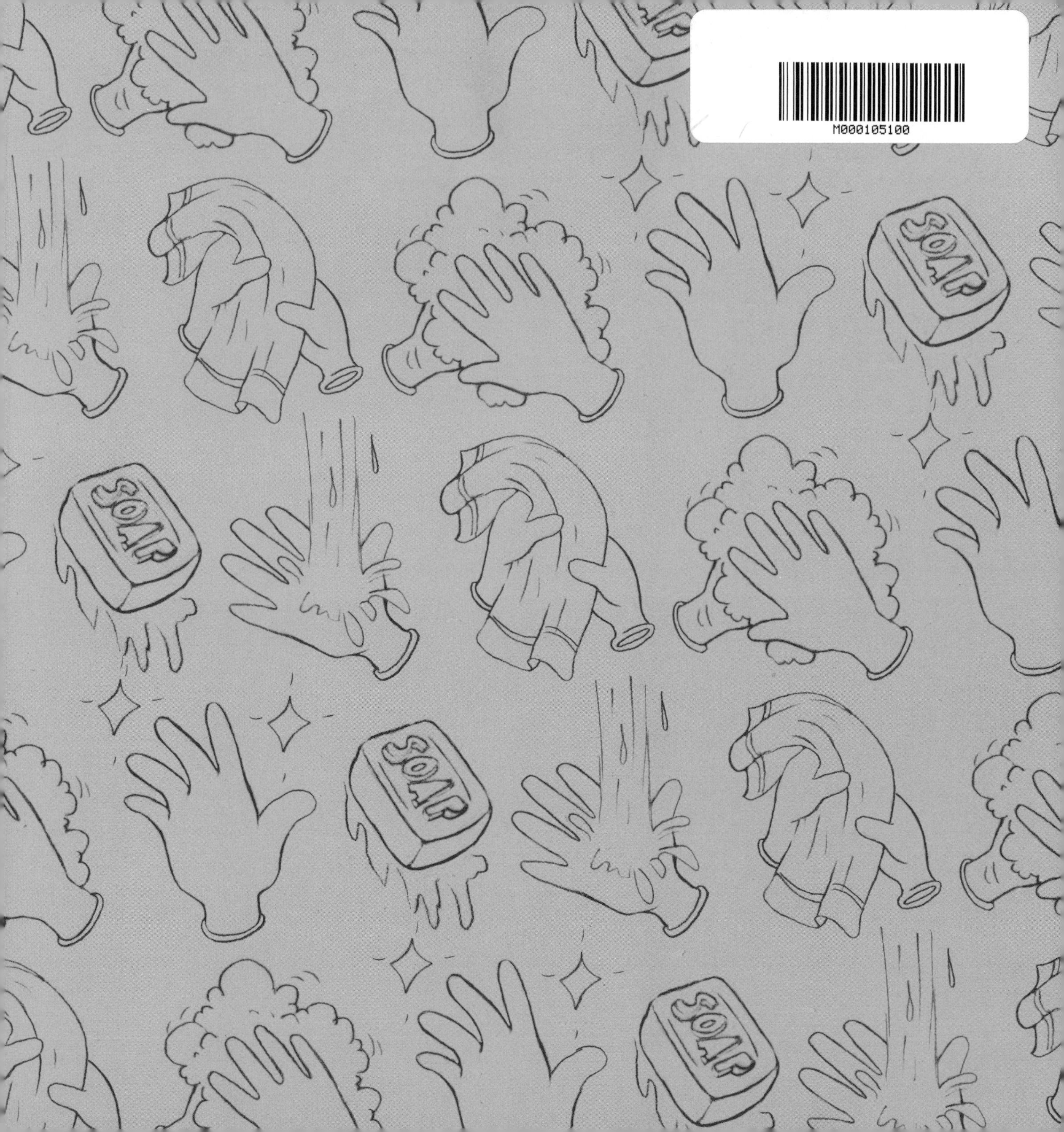
SOAP

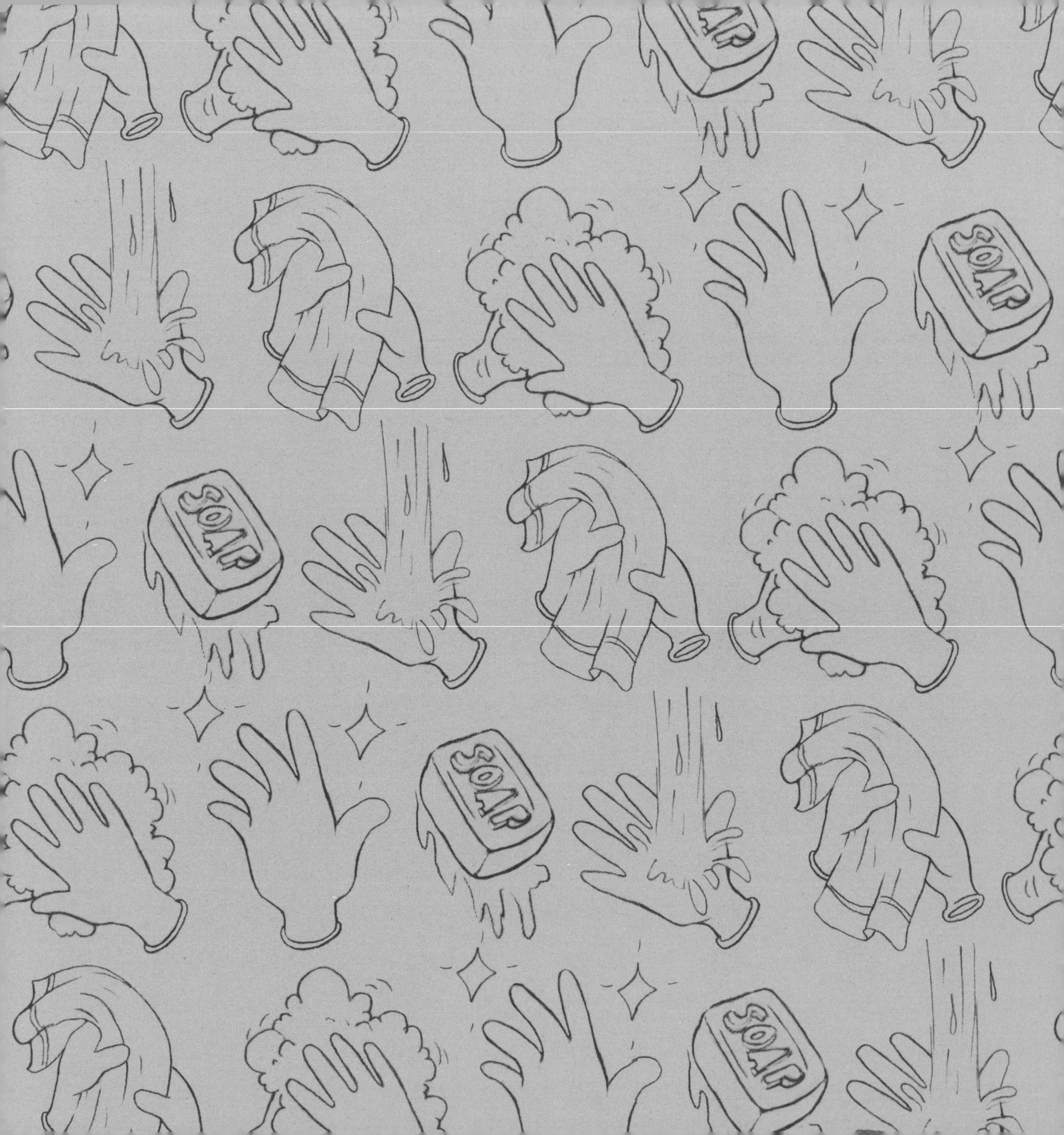
SOAP

The Soap Lady

by Renée French

www.topshelfcomix.com

French, Renée. 1963-
The Soap Lady/Renée French
[1. Picture Books. 2. Soap/Suds—Fiction. 3. Illustration.]

ISBN 1-891830-24-4
10 9 8 7 6 5 4 3 2 1

For my Mom.

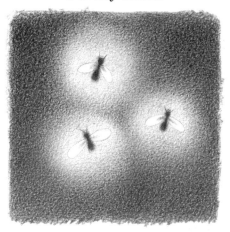

Thanks to Chris Staros, Brett Warnock, Gretchen Worden, the Mütter Museum, Penn Jillette, John Bloom, Arthur Penn, Maggie Raggaisis, Dave Cooper, Lisa Rosko, Paul Provenza, Jordan Crane, Craig Thompson, Scott Teplin, Tom Szymanski, Lil and Bill Gladding, Danny and Jen French, Anke Feuchtenberger, Jochen Enterprises, Piers Lauder, Teller, and Michael Goudeau. Rob, thank you for your love, support, and inspiration.

How many bunnies did you count? Write: bunnies@reneefrench.com

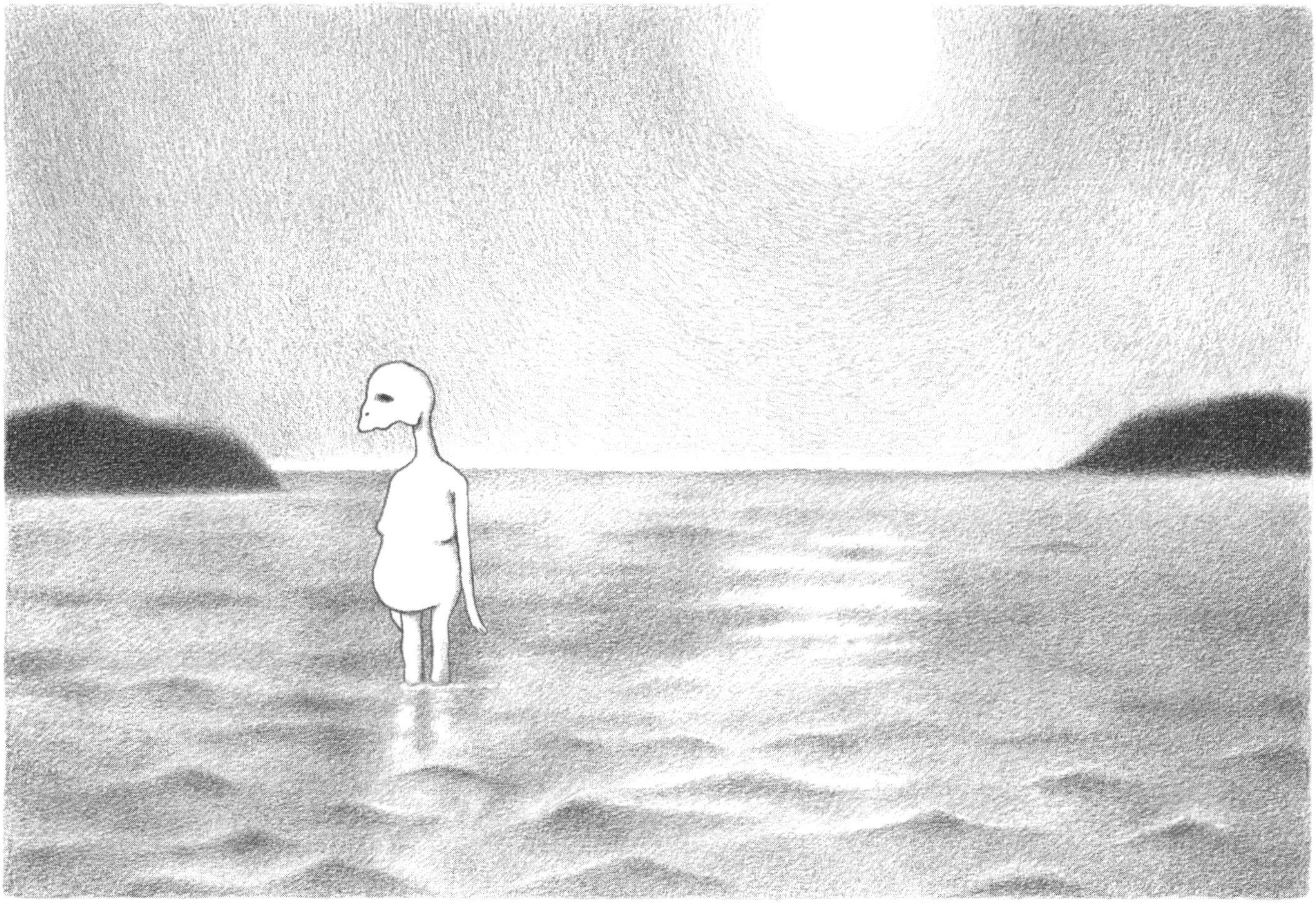

One morning...

...a lady, made entirely of soap, walked out of Snowflake Bay...

...and onto the shore of a town called Blinkerton.

The long journey to shore exhausted her...

...so she sat down to rest on a rock.

She'd barely had time to catch her breath
when she heard a cry from the woods.

Behind some trees she saw a little boy sitting in a pit of sludge.

"I'm in such humongous trouble," cried the boy.
"My mother's right, I can't stay clean for more than three minutes."

Just five days ago his mother had scolded him, "Look at you Rollo,
you're filthy again! If you could just stay clean for a week,
we'd get you that silly ventriloquist dummy you've always wanted."

"Oh no, now I'll never get that dummy," he sobbed,
"and I only had two more days to go."

Wanting to help, the Soap Lady walked over to the boy.

And as he pulled himself out of the sludge,
she tried not to look too intimidating.

16

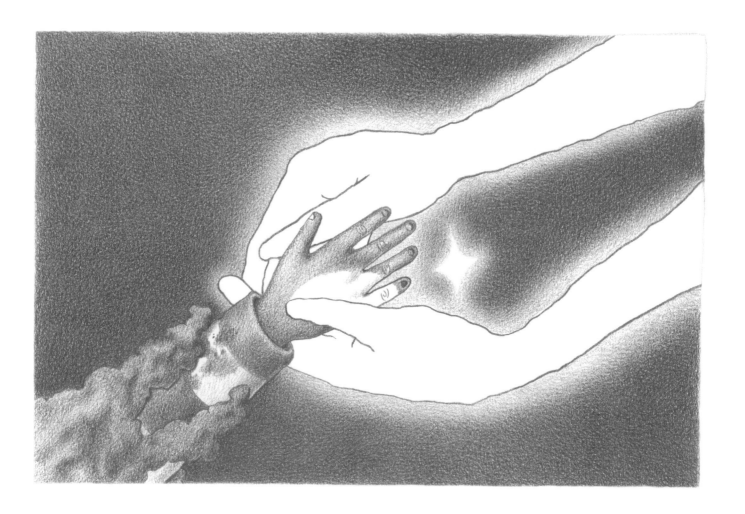

She took his hand and with one pass of her thumb, made it clean.

Then she did the rest of him.

Rollo was so clean he sparkled. "Thank you," he said.

The Soap Lady was delighted to help.

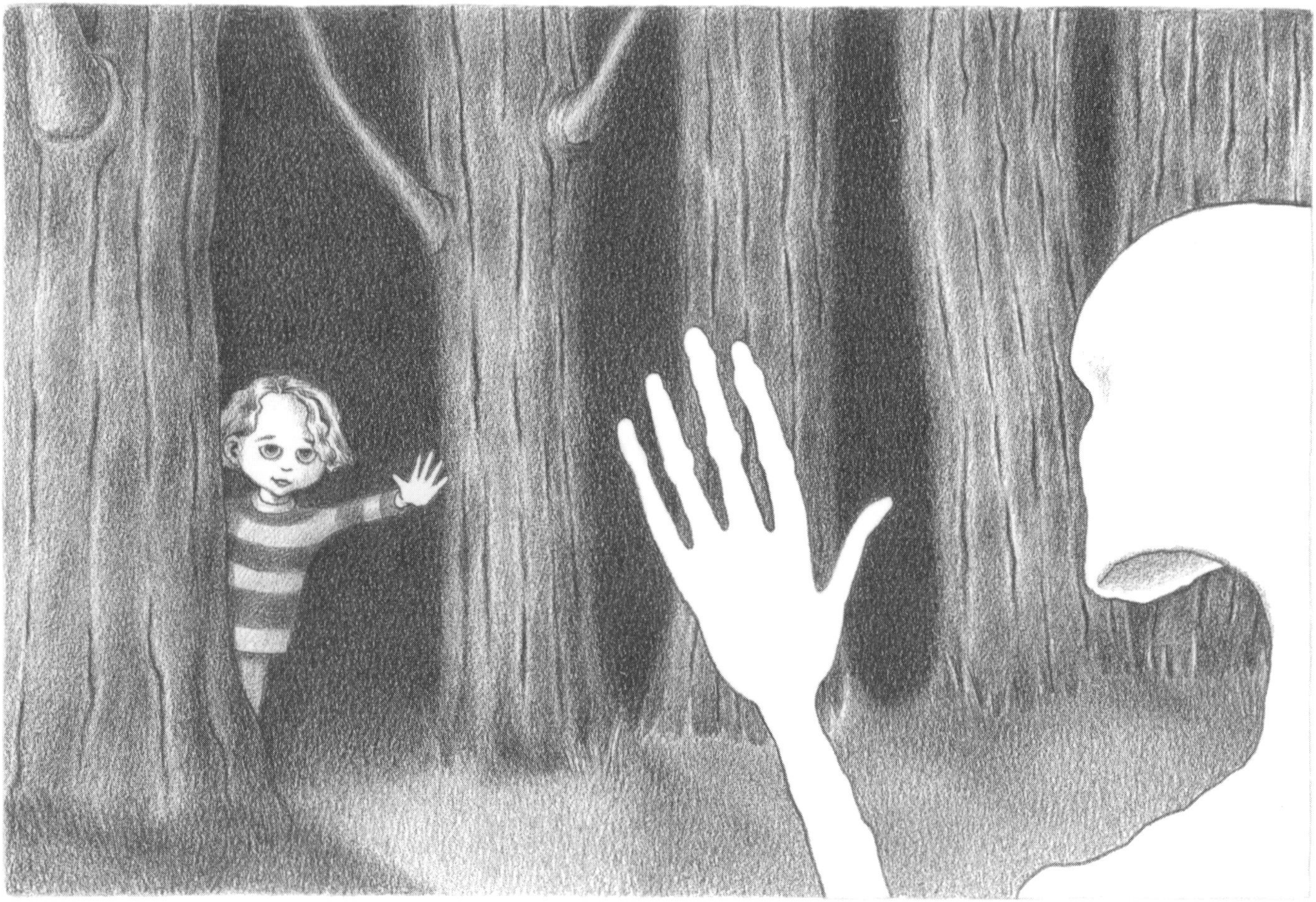

“I haven’t been this clean...ever!” Rollo exclaimed.
“Boy, will my Mom be surprised,” he said as he waved goodbye.

The Soap Lady was sorry to see him go.

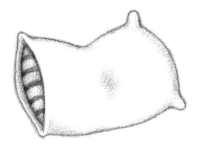

That night Rollo had a dream...

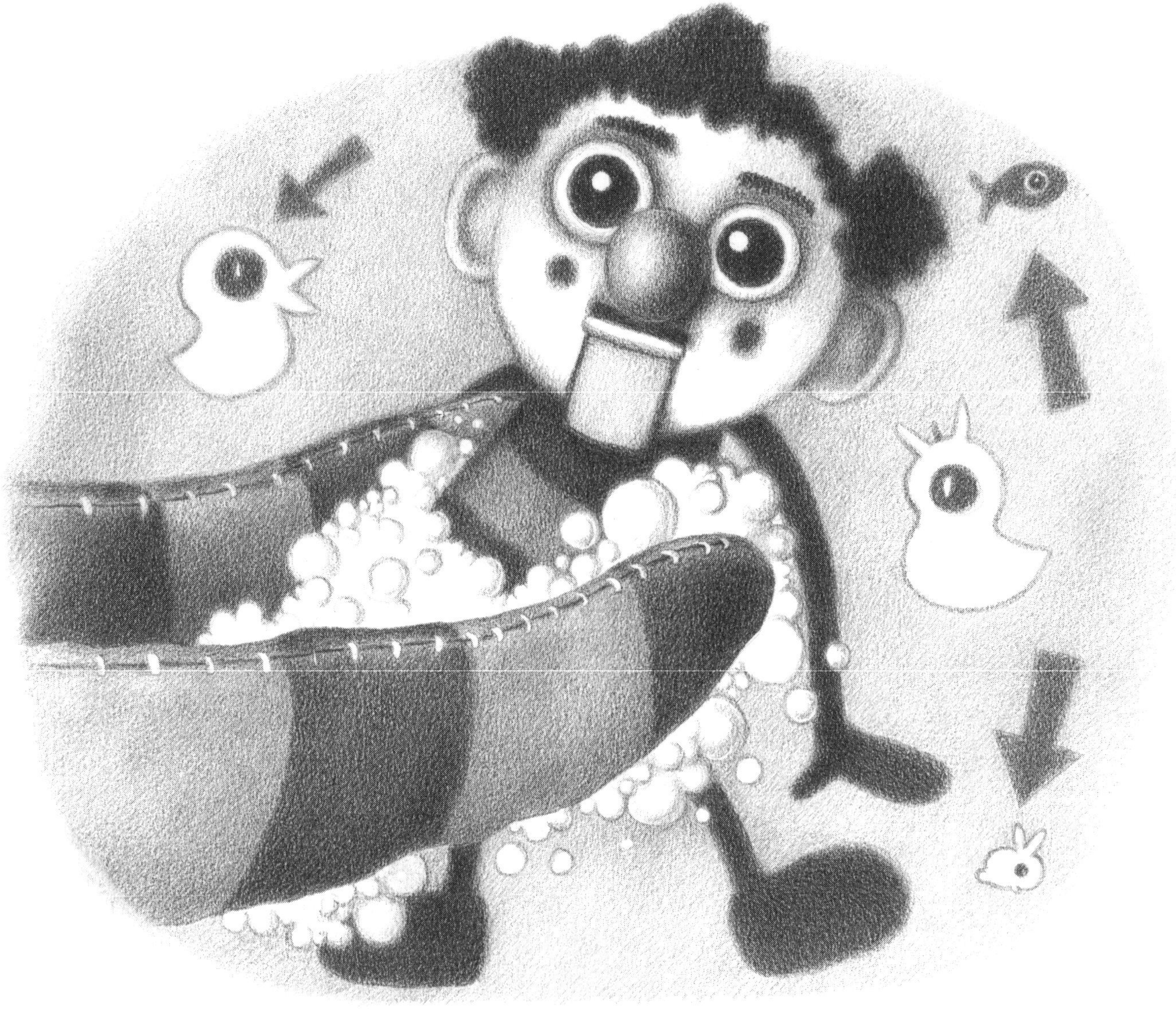

And the next day...

The Soap Lady spent her time cleaning things in the woods.

She walked and walked, looking for more things to clean.

She even did some creative cleaning...

...and then sat down to admire her work.

Just as she ran out of ideas,

Rollo emerged from the woods and said, "Hi."

"C'mon, let's play," Rollo said to the Soap Lady.

He took his new friend to the sheep field,
which was his favorite place in all the world.

And there the Soap Lady came up with an idea.

Before Rollo knew what was happening, she picked him up,
took a running start...

...and they slid down the hill on her slippery soapy back.
Rollo held on tight and giggled until his belly ached.

Later on, Rollo took the Soap Lady to his house.

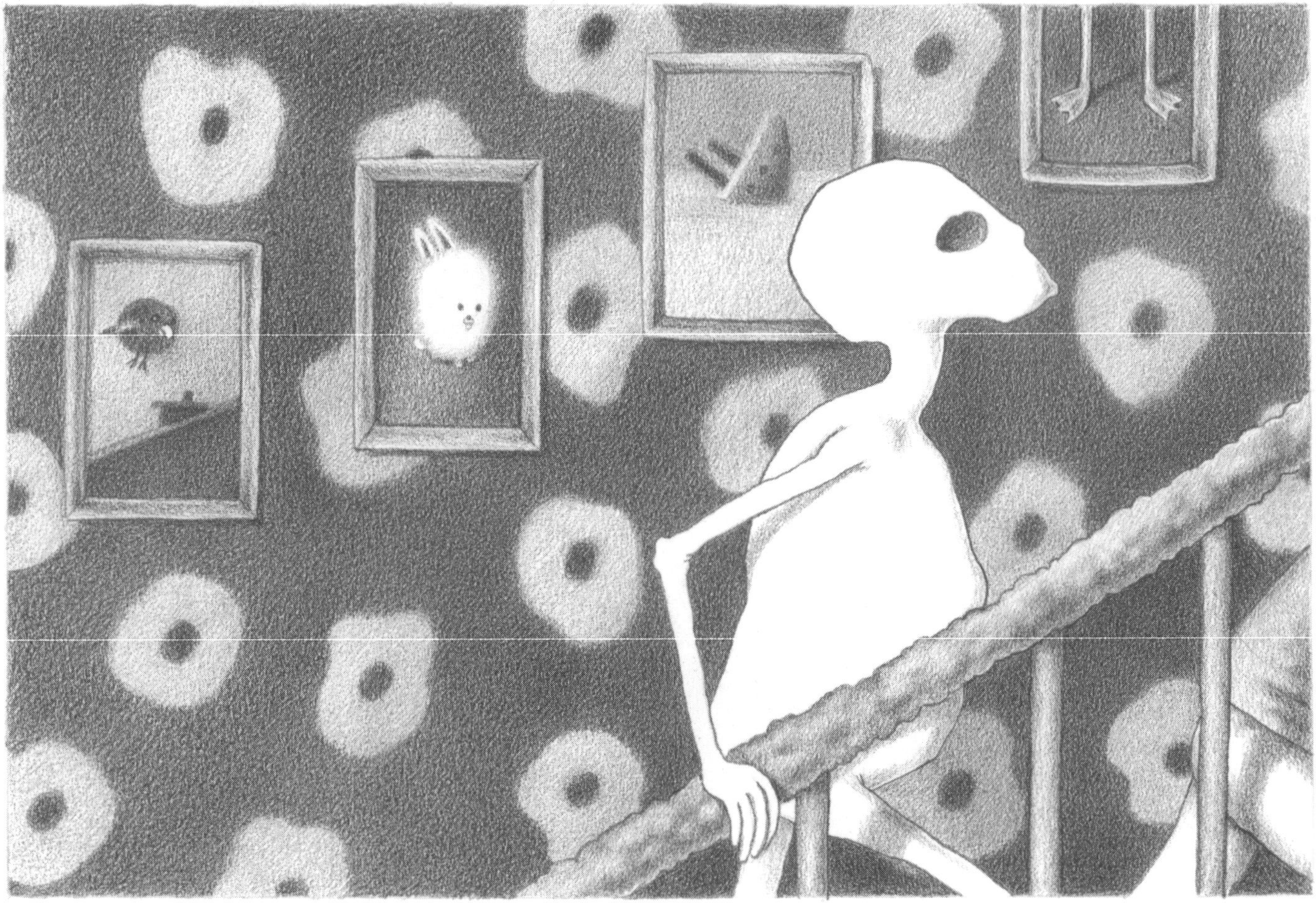

They went upstairs...

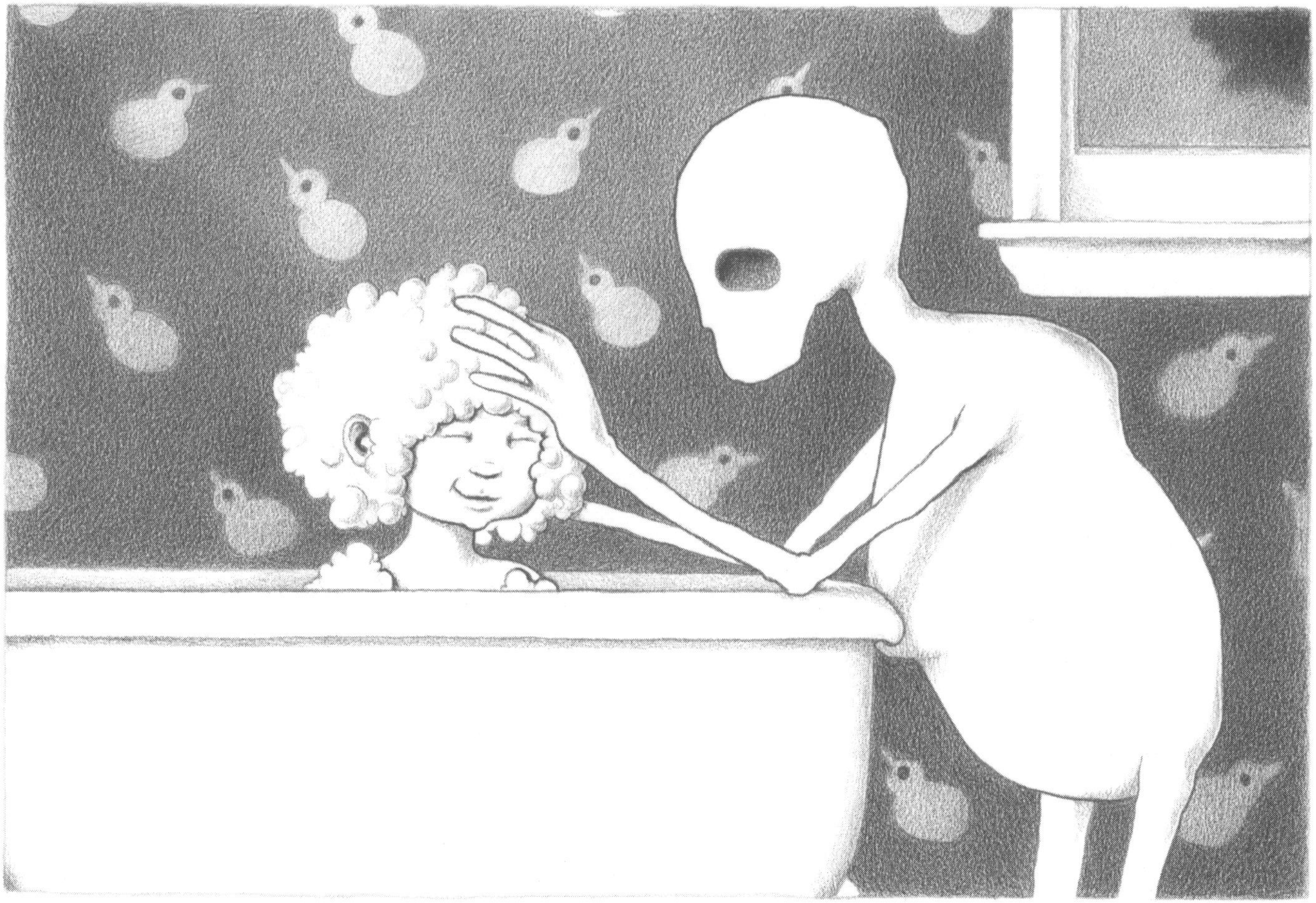

...and had some foamy fun.

Rollo was beginning to enjoy getting clean.

The next day...

...the Soap Lady decided to take a leisurely stroll around town.

She saw a little girl with chocolate on her face,
and with her finger she washed it clean.

"Stay away from my baby!" shrieked the girl's mother.

So the Soap Lady turned and sadly walked away.

"Hi," whispered Rollo.
The Soap Lady looked up and her sadness was gone.

"Look, isn't this dummy cool?"

The Soap Lady looked in the window and nodded.

Then she soaped the window and Rollo clapped with delight.

Rollo placed his hand in hers and they ran off to play together.

They found a fountain and the Soap Lady stuck her hand in the water...

...and let Rollo blow bubbles through her fingers. Lots and lots of bubbles.

After spending a sparkling day together...

...three boys from town showed up.

"Who's the freak, little man?" asked Oliver, the biggest boy.

"She's not a freak, Oliver. She's my friend," Rollo answered.

"Oh, I see, you're a freak-lover," sneered Oliver.
"Freak-lover, freak-lover," echoed the other boys.

"Please just leave us alone," Rollo pleaded.
"No, little man, I don't think we're gonna leave you alone.
You're a freak-lover, sissy-pants and your friend is an ugly monster."

All that name calling upset the Soap Lady,
so she decided to teach little Oliver a lesson.

She washed his mouth out with soap.

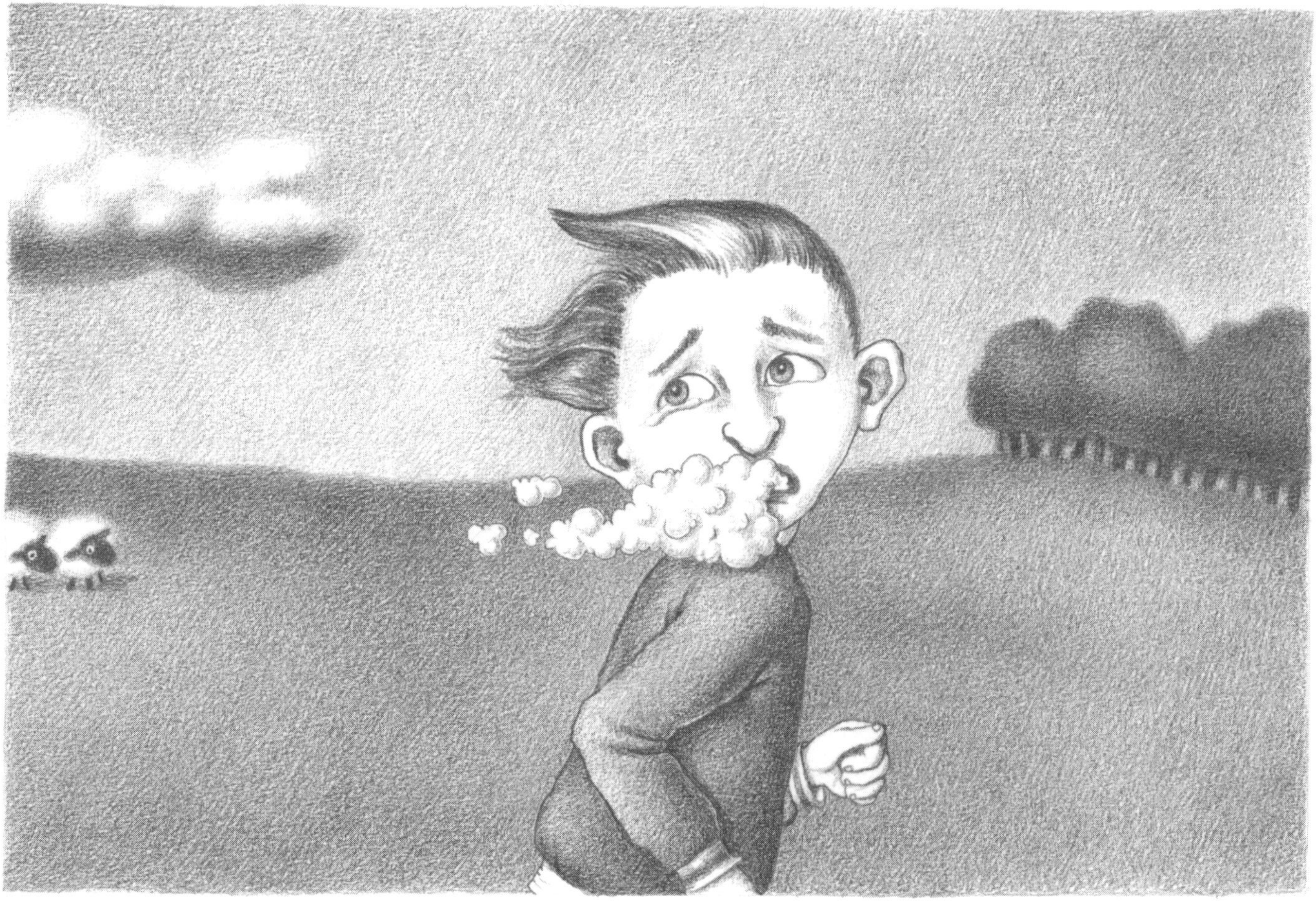

Oliver ran away...

...and Rollo gave the Soap Lady a big squeezy hug.

Oliver ran as fast as he could...

...straight to his Dad's butcher shop to tell him what had happened.

"There's a monster in the sheep field and it attacked me.
It's with Rollo right now!" he cried.

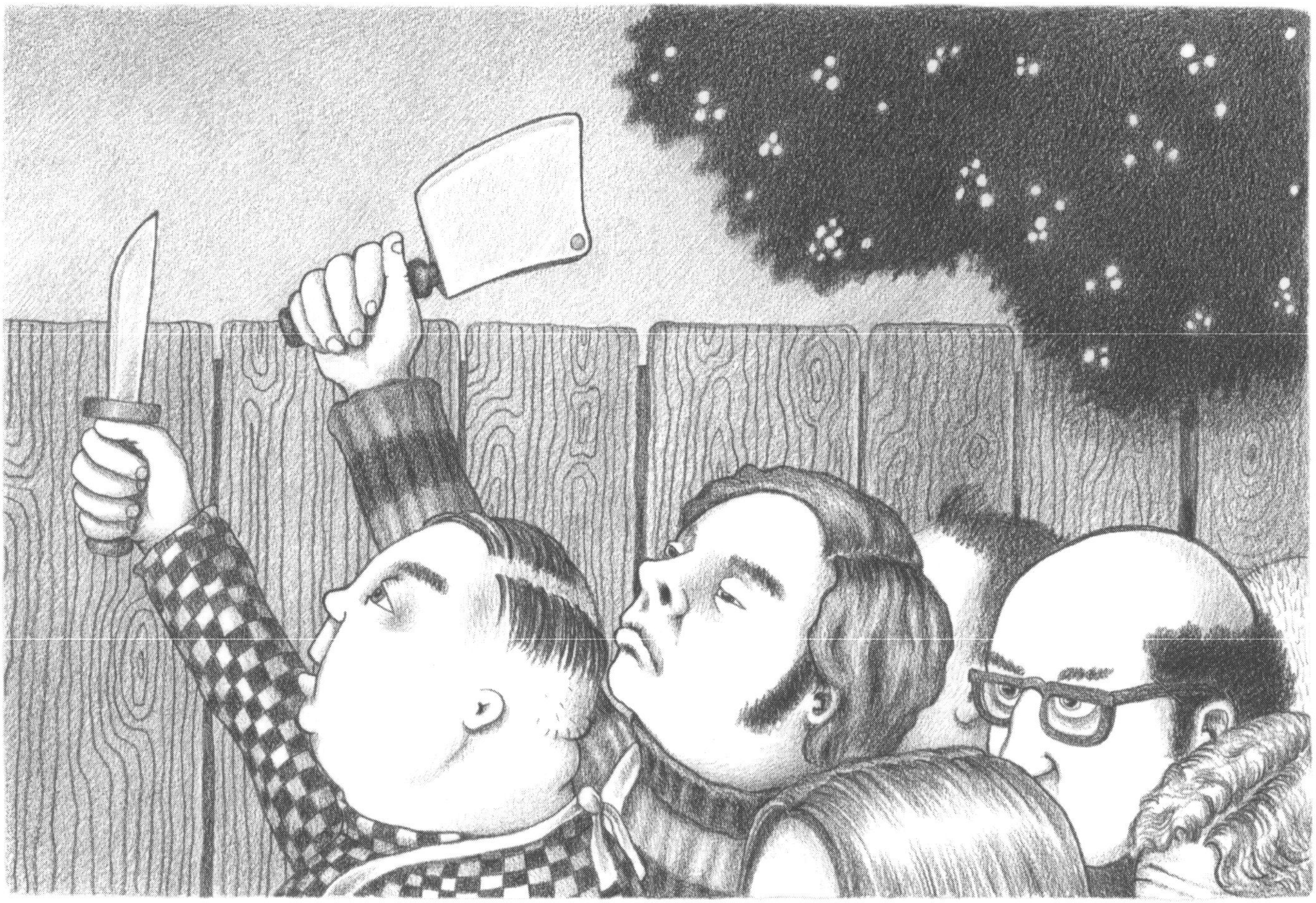

So Oliver's Dad assembled a group of townspeople and they marched right out to find the Soap Lady.

The angry mob searched the sheep field
but couldn't find the Soap Lady or little Rollo.

They were sitting by the water, watching the sun go down.

Then they heard the mob coming through the woods shouting,
"Get that monster!! Get that monster!!"

"Oh no!" said Rollo, "They're after you. You have to run away right now!"

The Soap Lady shook her head and Rollo insisted,
"They think you're a monster. They'll kill you if you stay."

The Soap Lady wiped away his tears.

"Get your mutant hands off that boy, you beast!" ordered Oliver's Dad.

"She's not hurting me. She's my friend.
Why don't you just leave us alone?" pleaded Rollo.

The Soap Lady knew she couldn't stay,
but wanted to be with Rollo nonetheless.

"Eewwwww! What the...?" said the mob.

So she gave Rollo a part of herself,
so he would always have soap to wash with.

"No! Let me go!" Rollo screamed, "Don't hurt her!"

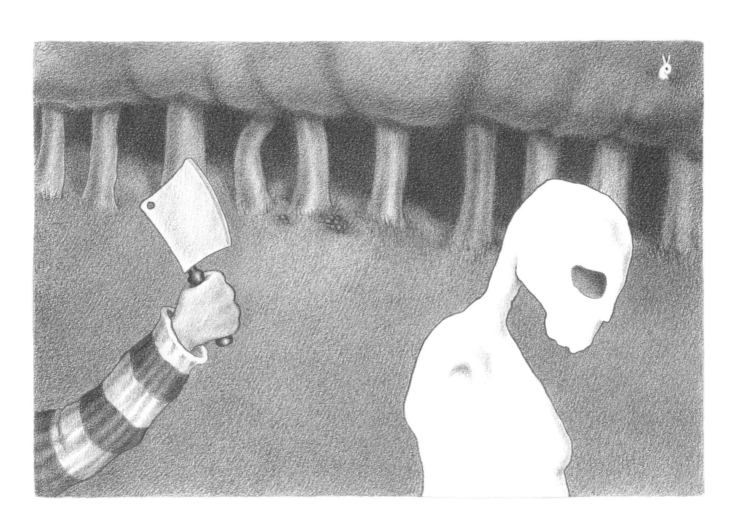

"Get out of here you monster!" yelled the mob.

So the Soap Lady made her way back to the bay.

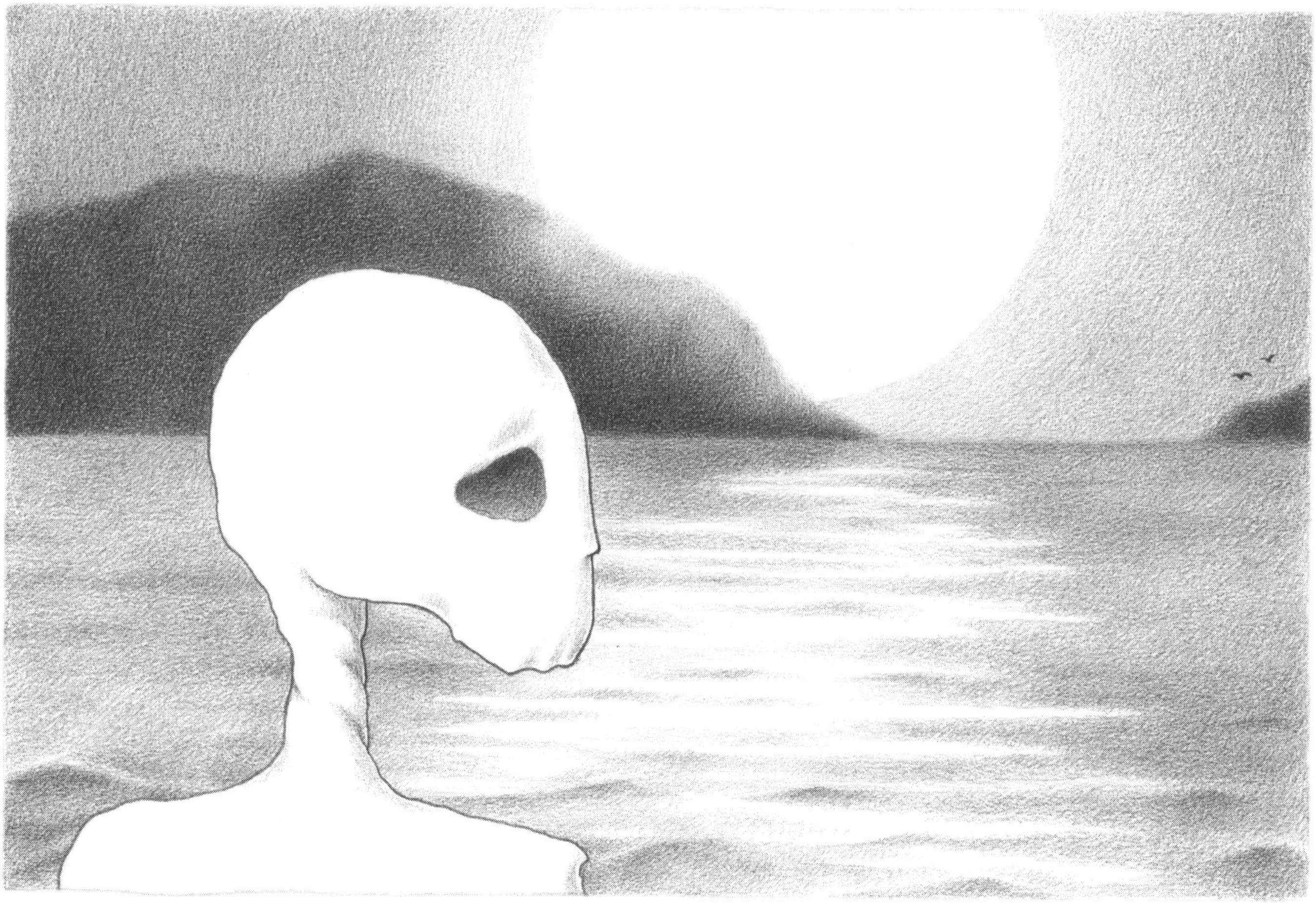

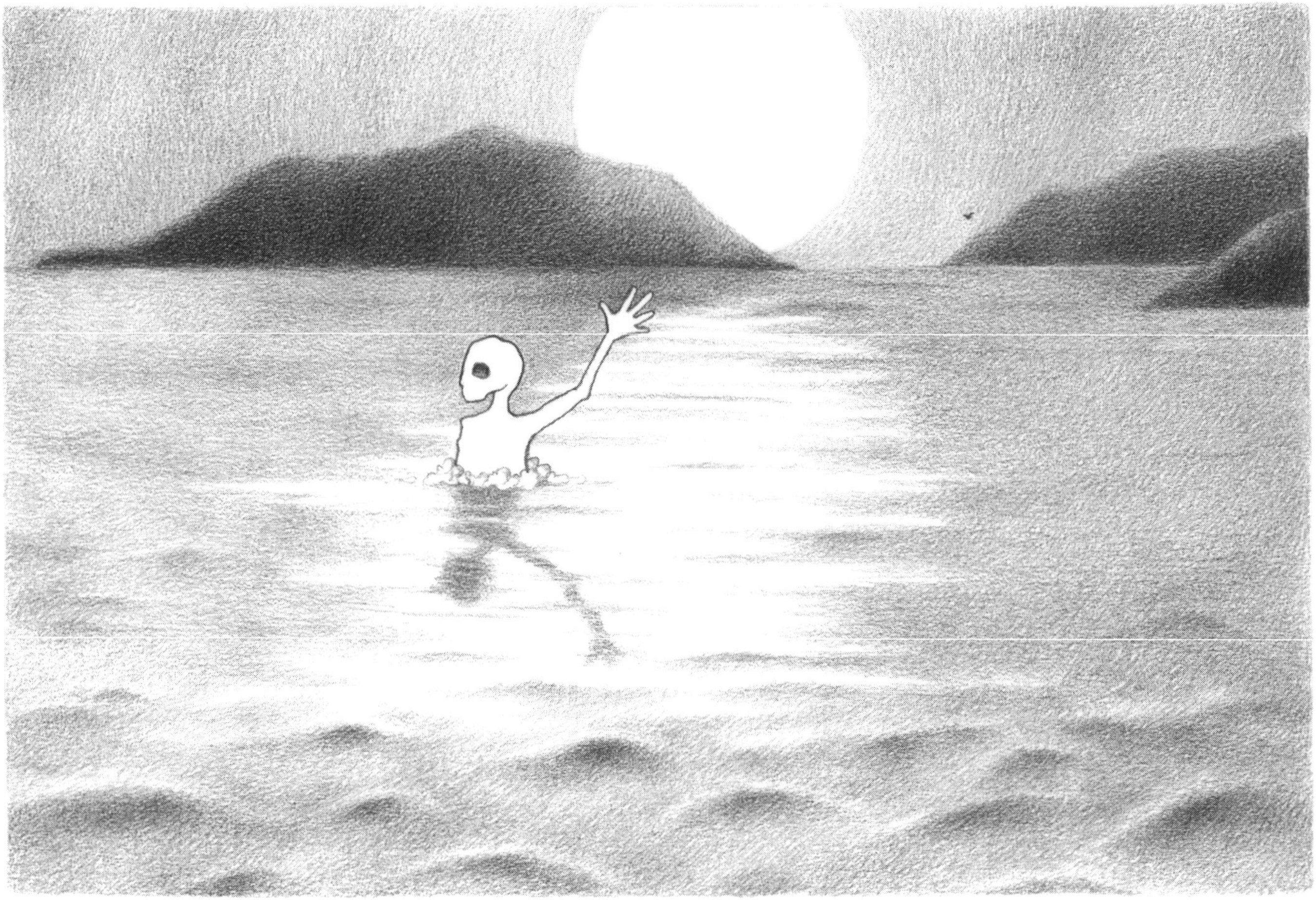

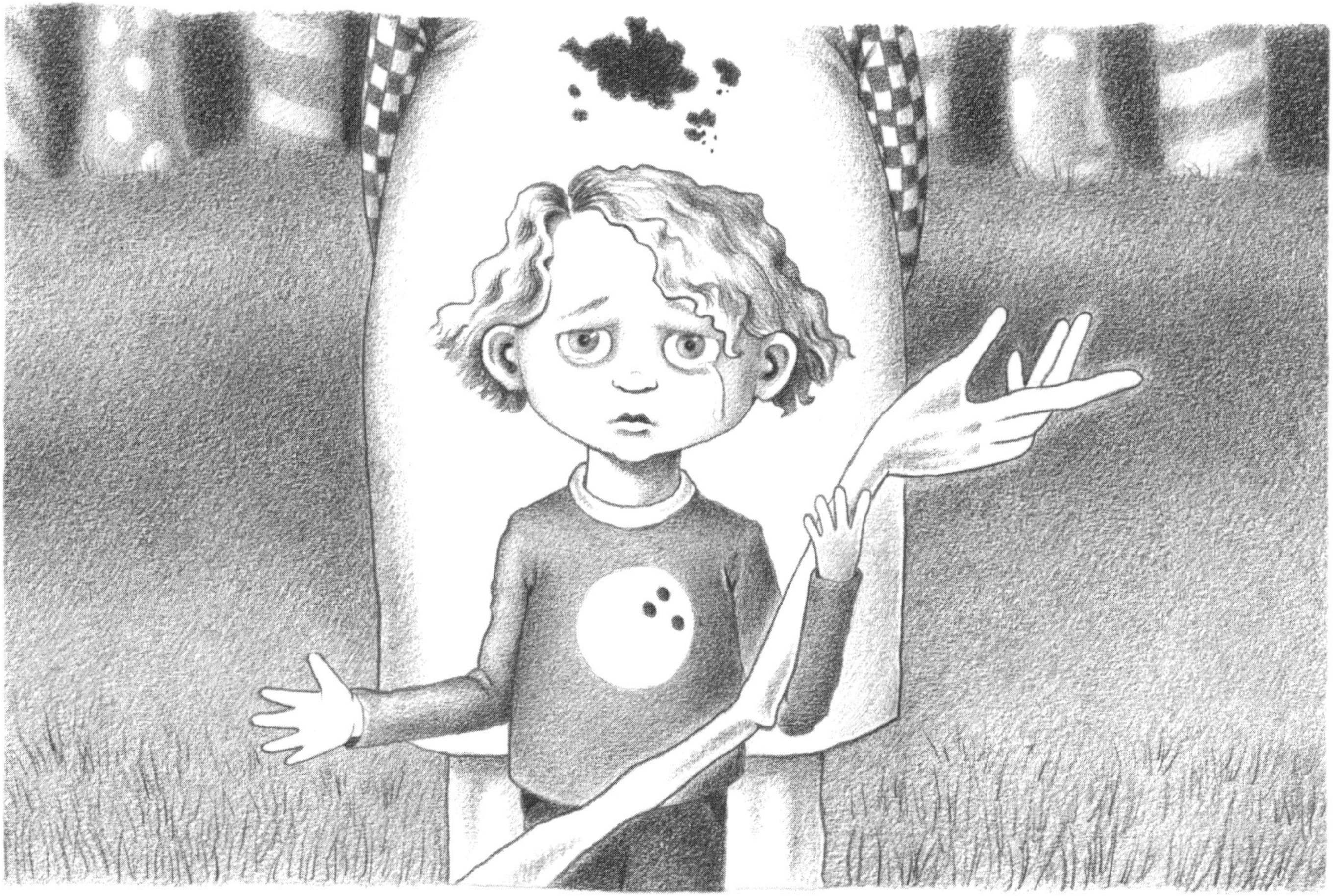

...

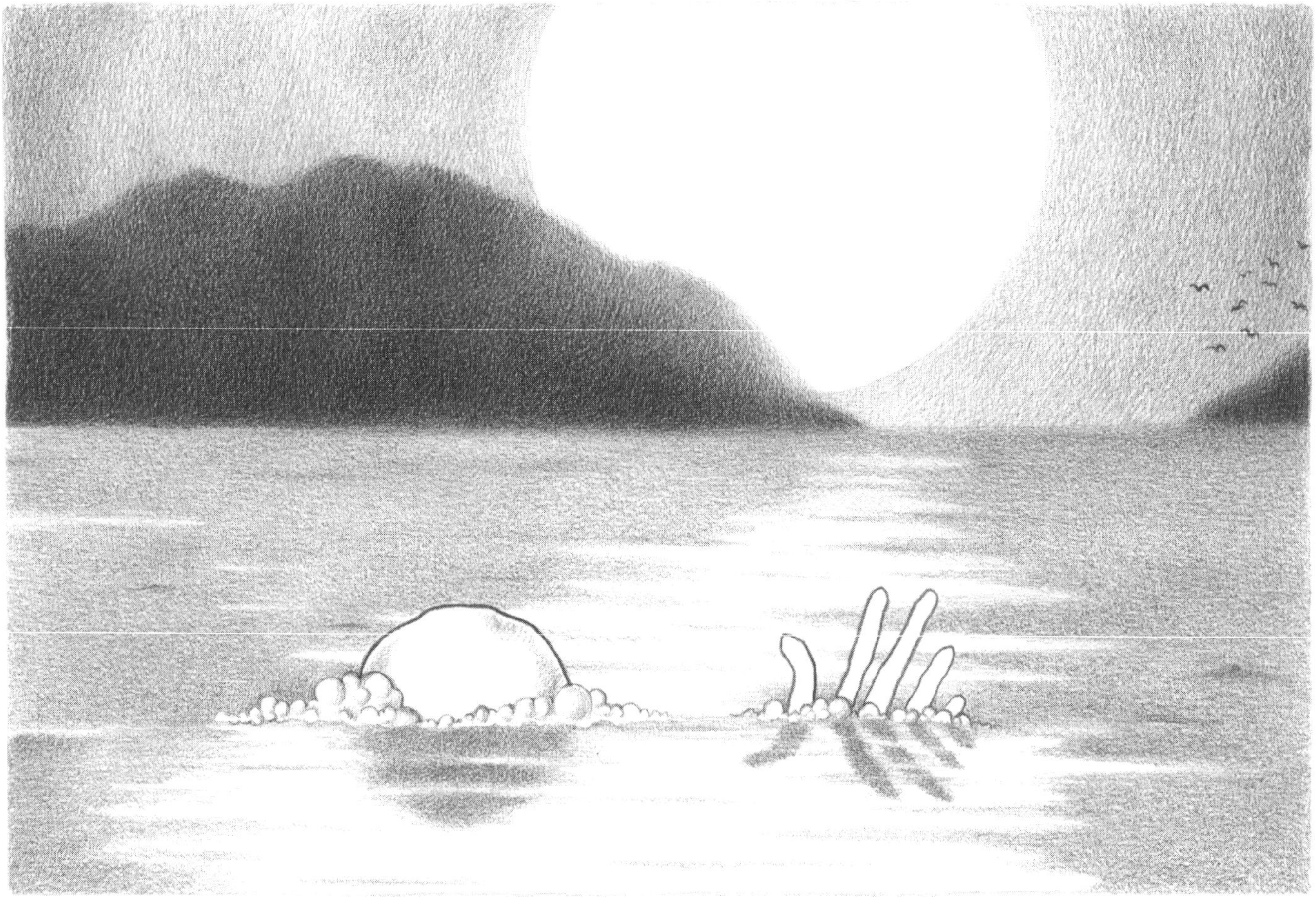

"Give me that," insisted Oliver's Dad,
as he grabbed the arm away from Rollo.

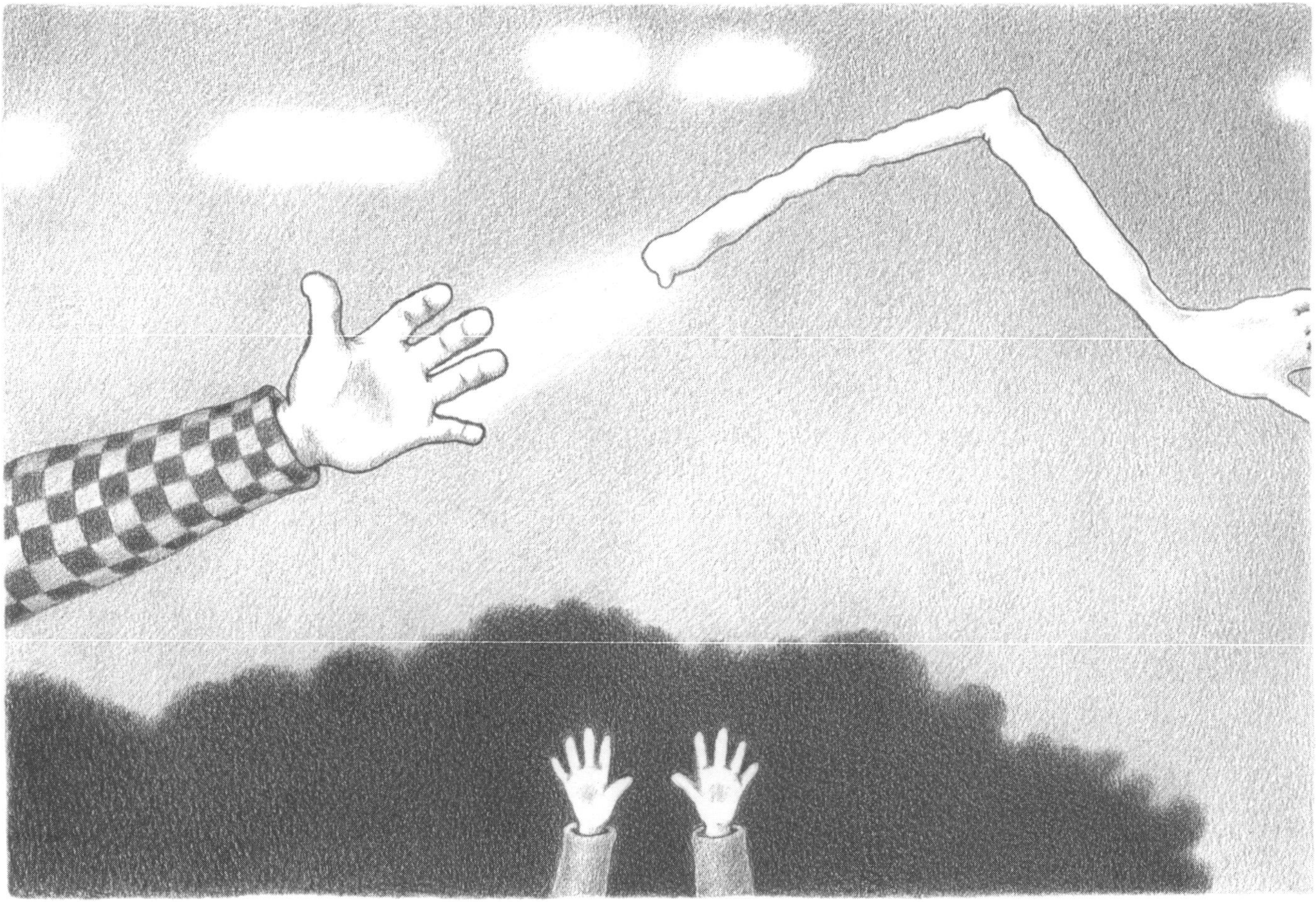

“Nooooooooo!” cried Rollo.

And Oliver's Dad threw the arm into the bay.

"Let's go home boys," said Oliver's Dad.

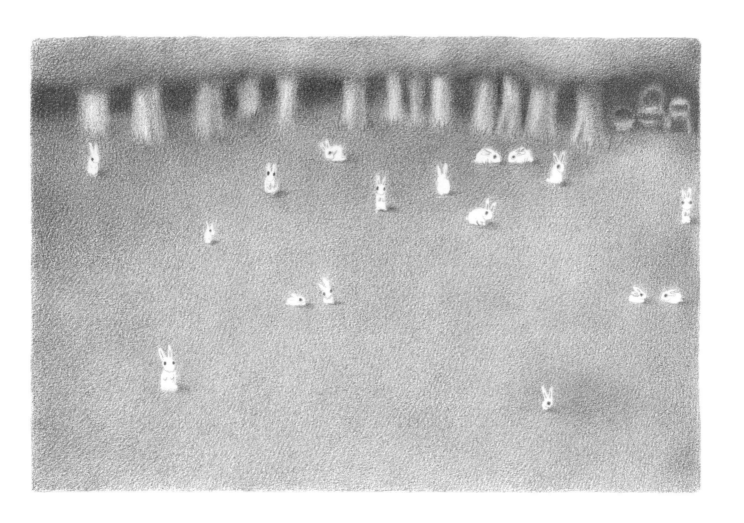

And the mob went home.

Rollo stayed by the water watching
the sun get closer and closer to the horizon.

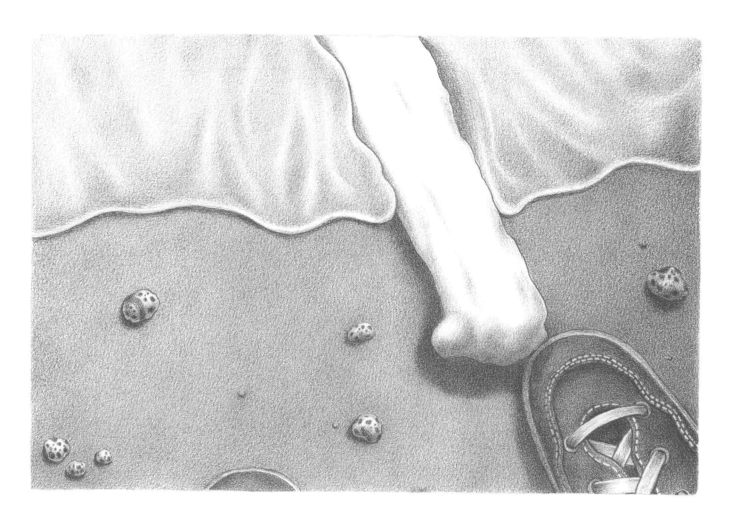

Then he felt something nudge his foot. It was the arm!

The Soap Lady was gone, but Rollo was not alone.

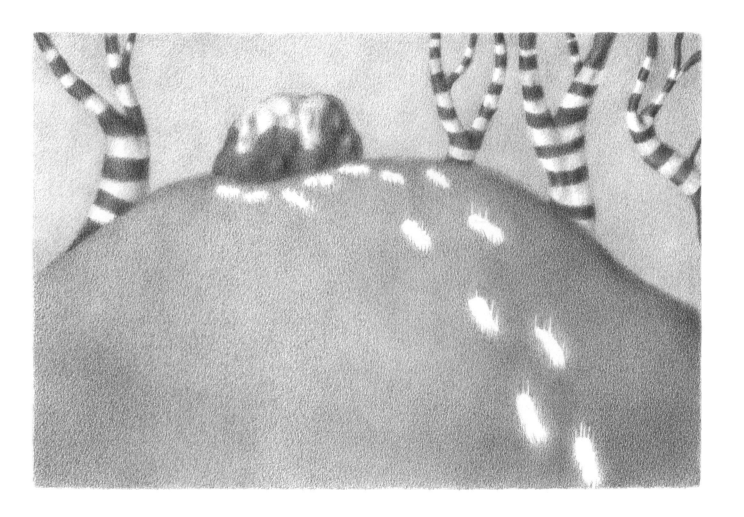

He had something to remember her by...

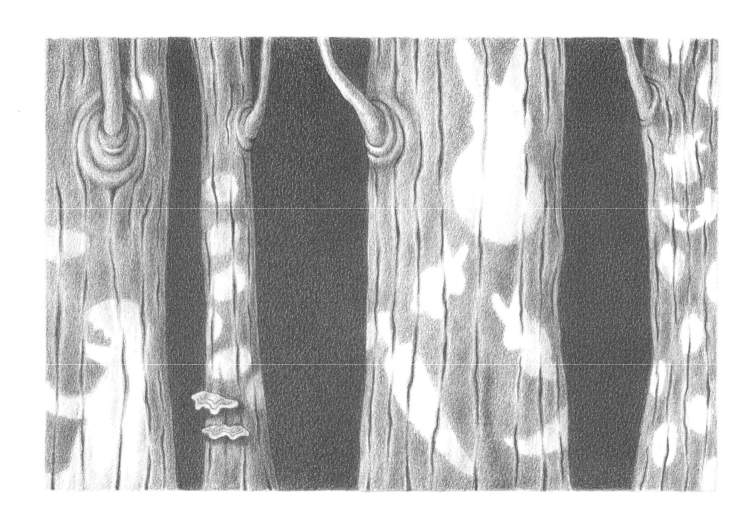

...and saw the Soap Lady everywhere he looked.

A few weeks later...

Rollo and Squeeker, the dummy, shared a bath.

"Are you in the tub, young man?" called Rollo's Mom from the kitchen.

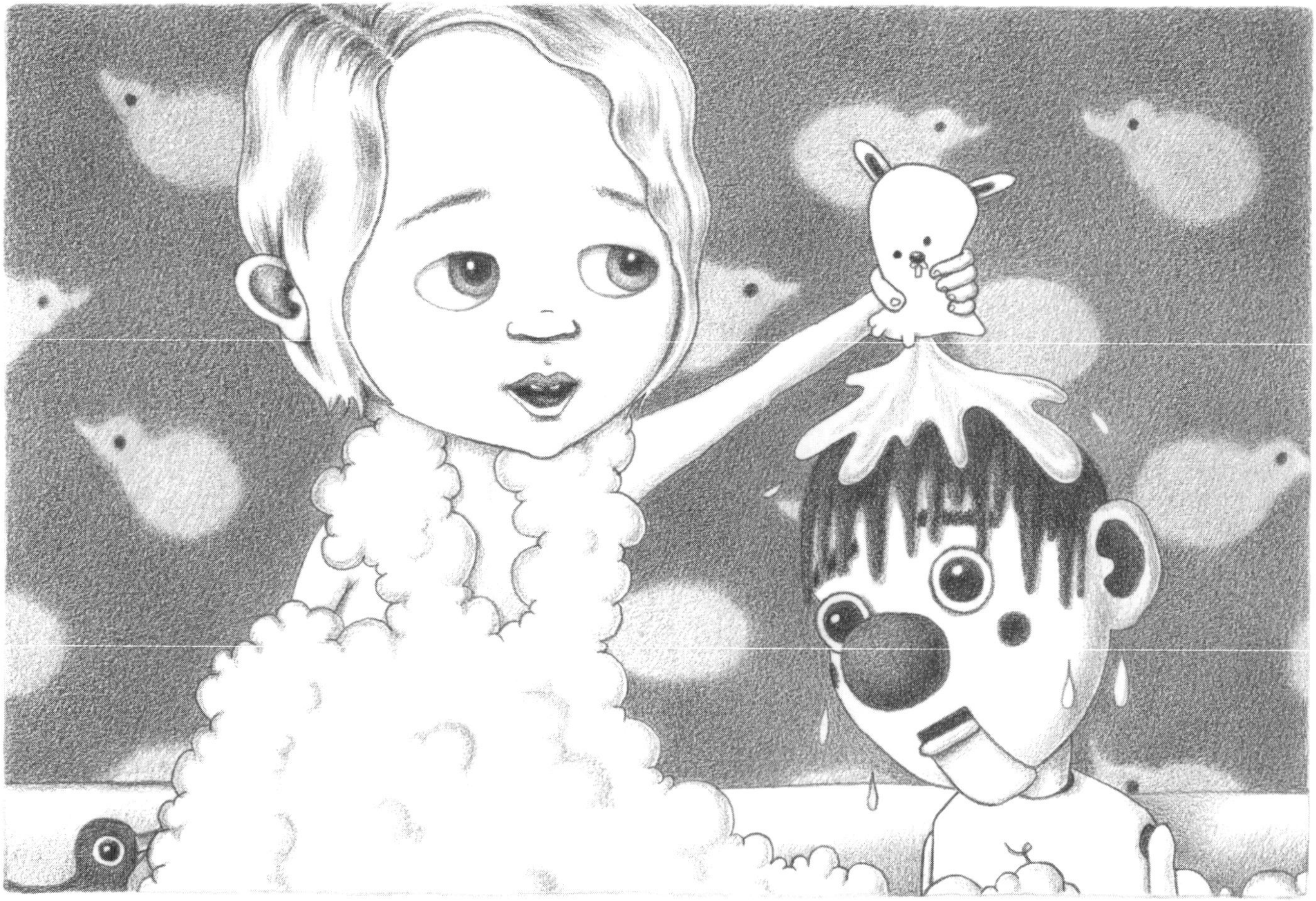

“Yes, Mom!” Rollo answered.

"I've got something really cool to show you, Squeeker," Rollo whispered.

Squeeker looked interested.

"It's something a friend taught me," Rollo continued.

The suspense must have been killing Squeeker.

"You just make an 'O', like this..."

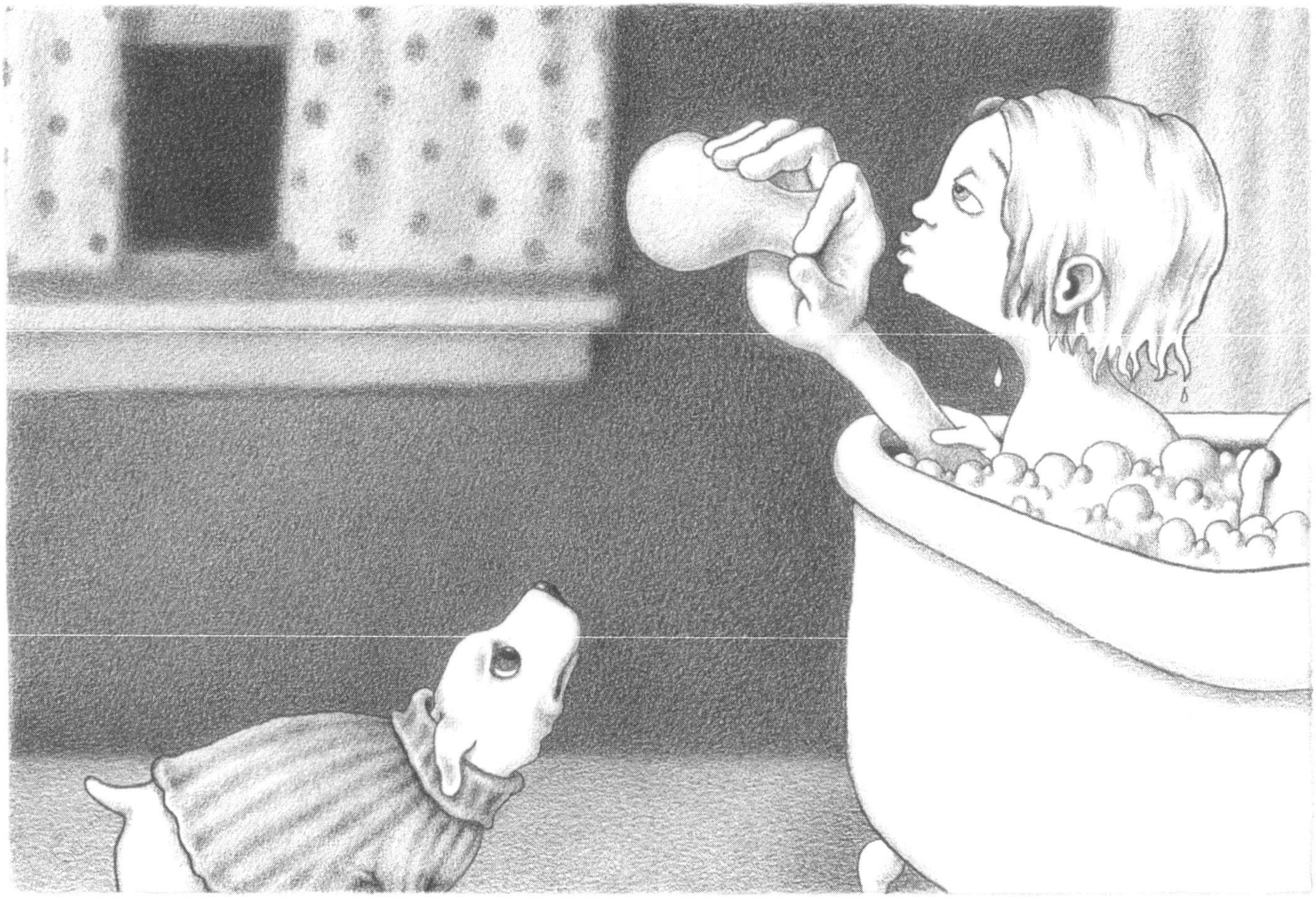

"...and..."

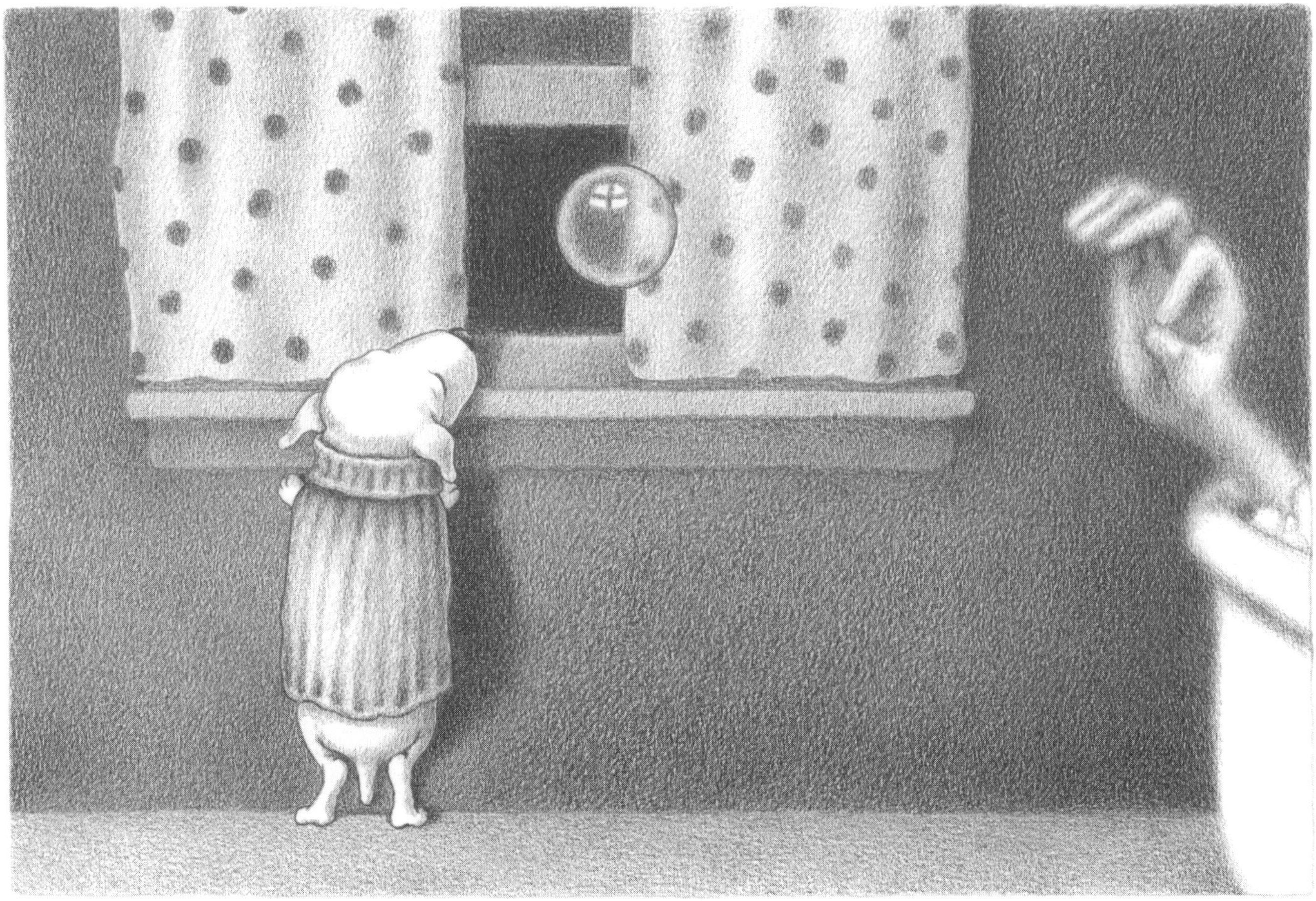

The breeze took it...

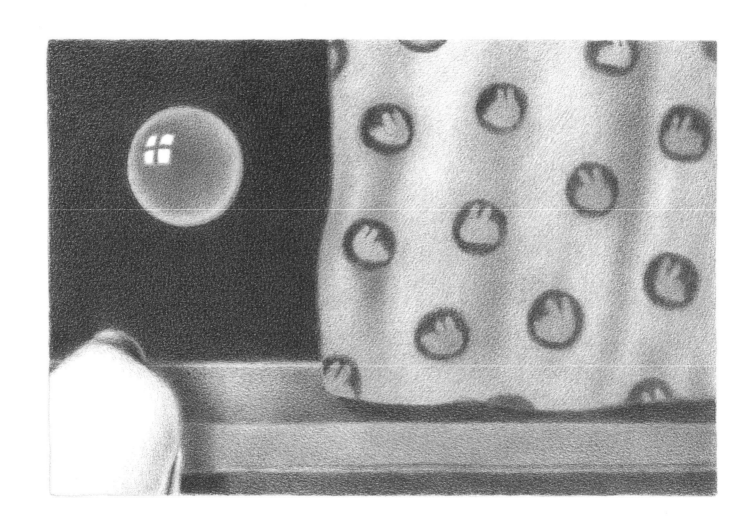

...for a leisurely stroll...

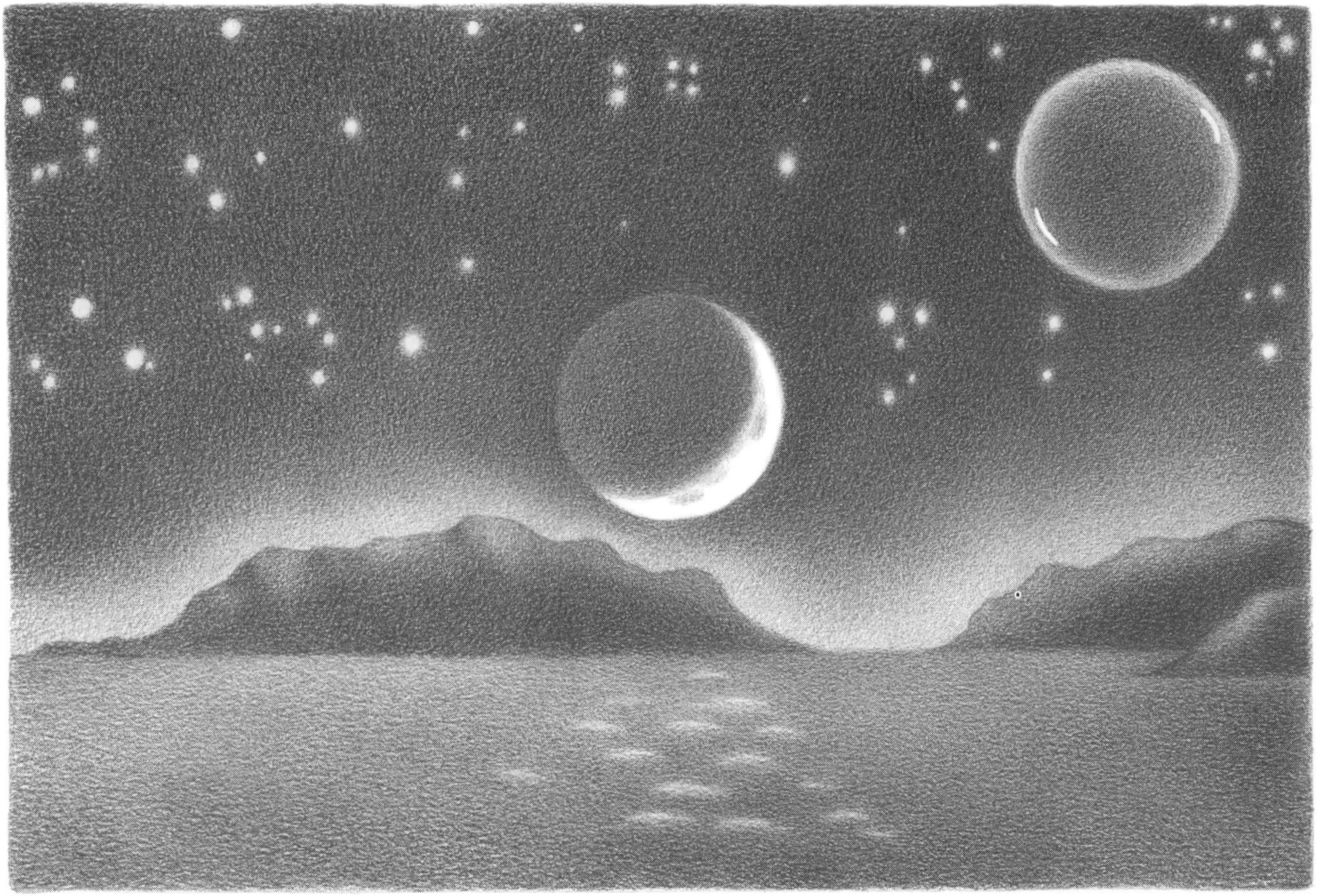

...across the bay.

In December 1874, the well-preserved body of a woman was found in a Philadelphia cemetery that was being relocated. Her fat had turned to adipocere, a waxy substance similar to lye soap that can occur in fat tissues under certain burial conditions. A Philadelphia physician, Dr. Joseph Leidy, recognized the scientific significance of this form of natural preservation, and got permission to send her body to the Mütter Museum of the College of Physicians of Philadelphia. Evidence from X-rays of her skeleton and from pins used to fasten a shroud around her suggests that when she died sometime in the 1830's or 1840's, she was around 40 years of age. We still do not know who she was or why she died, but further investigation may one day reveal the answers to some of these questions.

She can be seen on display at the Mütter Museum in Philadelphia at the College of Physicians of Philadelphia.

—Gretchen Worden, Director, Mütter Museum

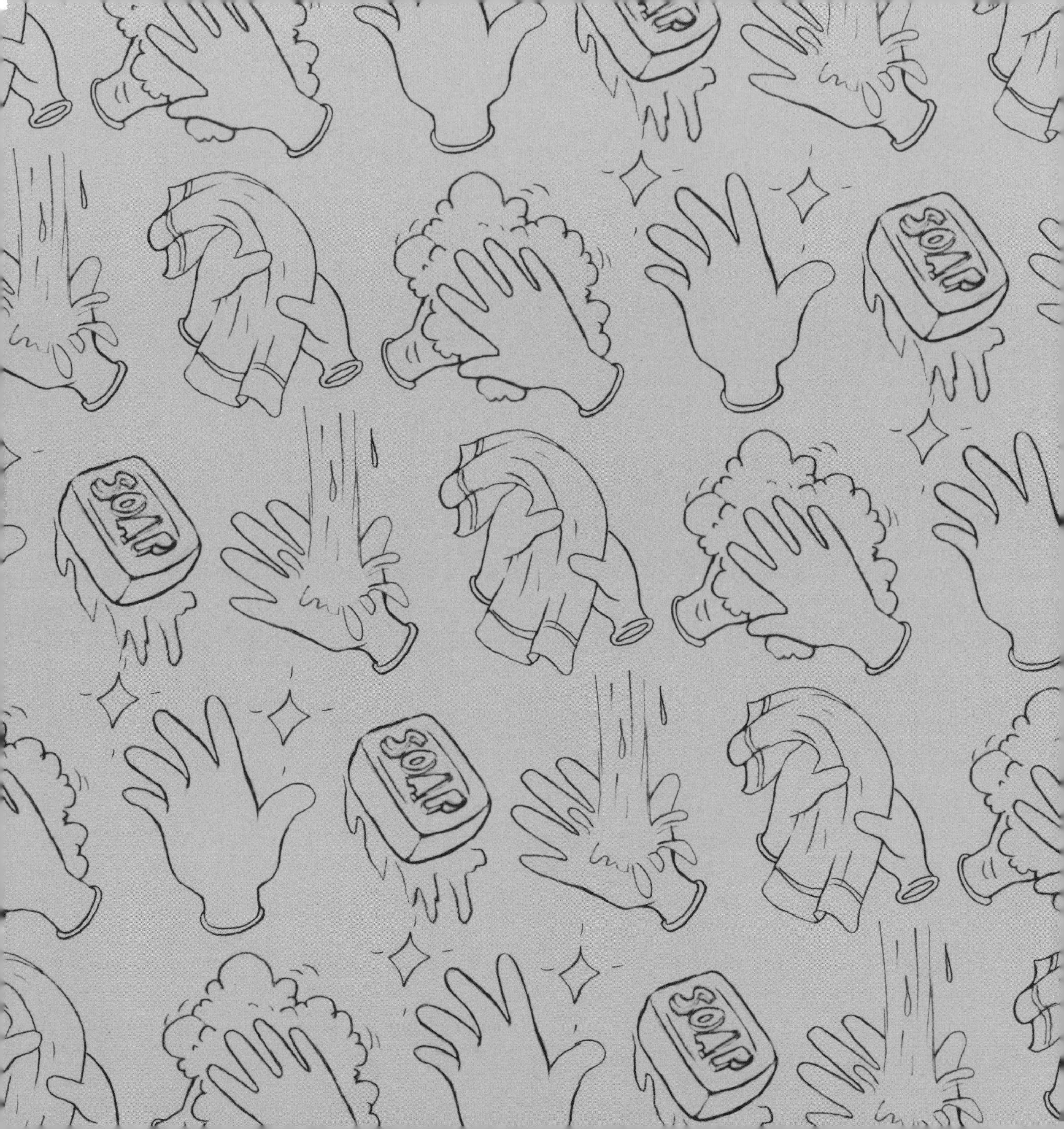
SOAP
SOAP
SOAP
SOAP

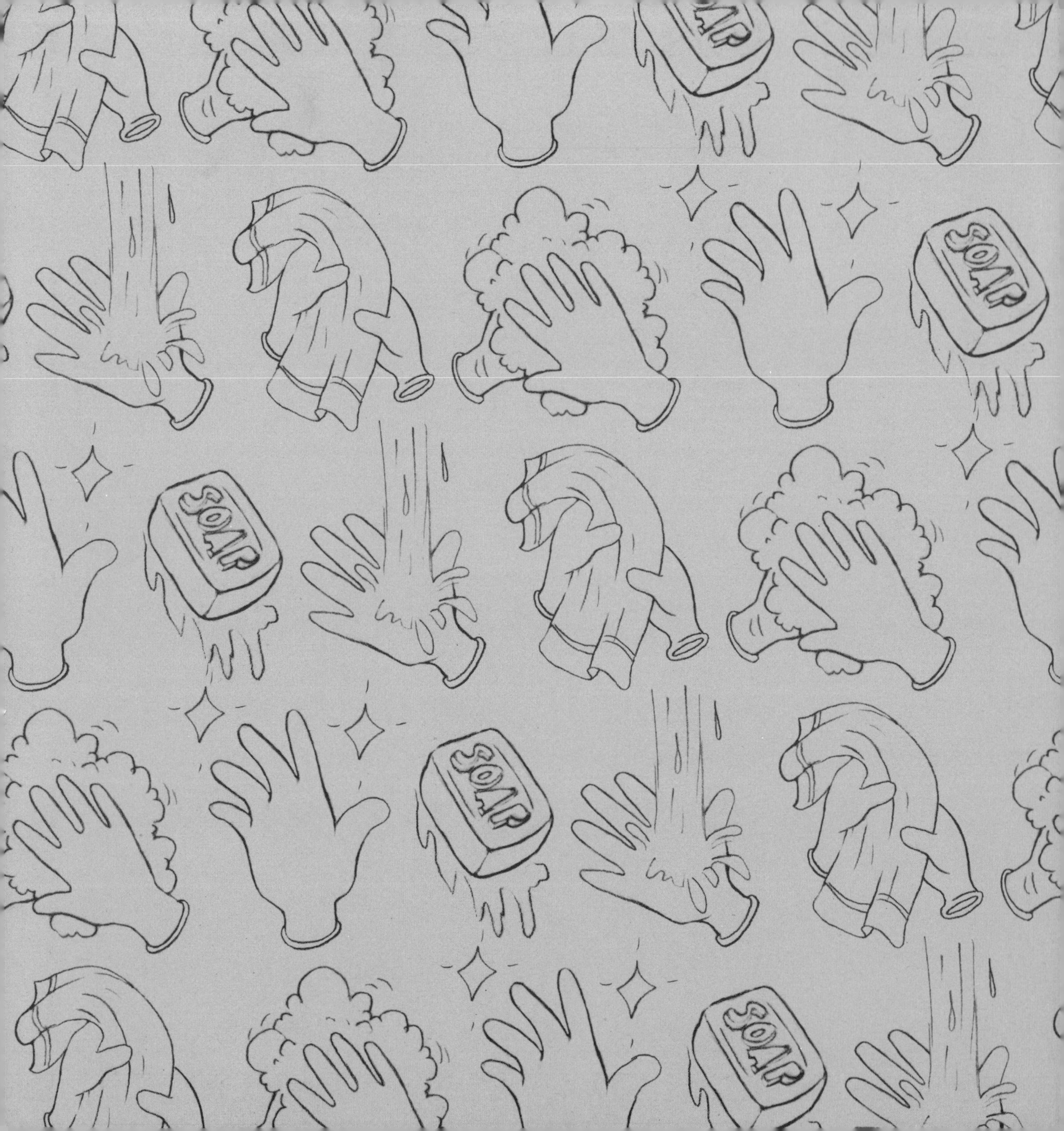
SOAP
SOAP
SOAP
SOAP